FISHING FOR DOGS

BY DICK BERNAL

FISHING FOR DOGS

ISBN# 13-978-0692931820

Printed in the United States of America

Published by
Jubilee Christian Center
175 Nortech Parkway
San Jose, California 95134
www.jubilee.org

CONTENTS

"Follow Me,
and I will
make you
fishers of men."

— Matthew 4:19

Me at 2.

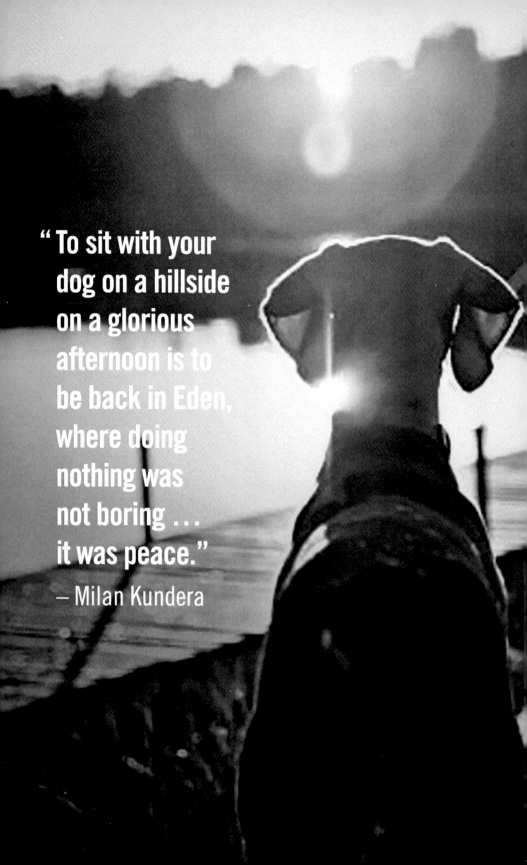

" To sit with your dog on a hillside on a glorious afternoon is to be back in Eden, where doing nothing was not boring ... it was peace."

— Milan Kundera

INTRODUCTION

HA! Admit it! The title of this book got you somewhat curious. Hopefully, if you read a little further, it will make sense, maybe even provoke some new ways of thinking how better to reach people with this beautiful story of Jesus. Let's face it, religion and politics can be polarizing and have ruined more than one family gathering... at least in my case.

Growing up back in the fifties in rural Watsonville, California, I had the blessing of living next to Pinto Lake. It's a smallish lake, but to a kid, it was paradise. Pinto Lake was full of bass, crappie, and bluegill fish. At six years of age, I became quite the skilled little fisher-boy. I made my own pole. Used string for my fishing line, and even made my own hooks out of safety pins. Grandma would save old Campbell soup cans so I could dig worms for bait. So, I was ready.

I caught so many bluegills, and of course, I wanted Grandma to cook them up. She begged me to *bless our neighbors*. Some accepted my fish-gift, others simply said, "No thanks, Dickie, but how sweet." Thank God Grandpa liked eating bluegill, so it was us two fellas out-voting Grandma.

Not only did I love to fish; like most boys, I loved dogs. Before I get too far along, let me back up a bit and paint a better picture of living off Dick Phelps Drive in Watsonville.

The little street we lived on was named after my uncle, my mom's only brother, who died in 1941, at the age of twenty, while saving an eighty-year-old lady's life in a freak Southern California flash flood. It was Grandma Lou and Grandpa Bill's only son. I came along in 1944, and I was named after Uncle Dick. He gave his young life to save an old soul at the end of her life. Saving people seems to run in our family, perhaps in some way because of Uncle Dick.

Mom and my two sisters, Judy and Juanita, lived next door to Grandma and Grandpa. Mom and Dad got divorced when I was around three, so I have no memories of him being a daddy to us kids in Watsonville. With my two sisters in school and Mom working many hours at Fords Department Store down on Main Street, Grandma and Grandpa helped raise me. Living side-by-side was cool because I could still play with my sisters, see Mom, but sleep over at my grandparents.

Ok so why such a strange title for this little book? Early in the first Gospel, we see this:

"And Jesus, walking by the Sea of Galilee, saw two brothers, Simon called Peter, and Andrew his brother, casting a net into the sea; for they were fishermen. Then He said to them, "Follow Me, and I will make you fishers of men." (Matthew 4:18-19)

My first year as a Christian was in 1977. I loved all the fishing passages in the Gospels. From 1977 to 1980 Carla, baby Sarah, and I lived up in Paradise, California, about 160 miles Northeast of the Bay Area.

I was an ironworker back then with territory from the Oregon border to Sacramento. So, loving fishing and hunting, we moved to the little Hamlet of Paradise, nestled in the Sierra Foothills due east of Chico in Butte County.

Paradise was a rock's throw from Lake Oroville, one of California's biggest lakes and any fisherman's dream. There were times I would take my twelve foot Klamath boat, my dog, a bag of chips, and go catch fish after work while Carla cooked dinner. It was a short drive to the boat ramp at the very northern end of Lake Oroville.

Many times, I would take my Living Bible (my first) and read the Gospels, always smiling at the fishing references, especially Peter's miracle catch, or the time they needed tax money, and Jesus said basically, leave your nets at home and grab your pole. I have cleaned hundreds, if not more, fish but never found a gold coin... but I keep hoping!

Ok, how do dogs fit in this picture? Let's look at this passage of scripture:

> "Then Jesus went out from there and departed to the region of Tyre and Sidon. And behold, a woman of Canaan came from that region and cried out to Him, saying, "Have mercy on me, O Lord, Son of David! My daughter is severely demon-possessed." But He answered her not a word. And His disciples came and urged Him, saying, "Send her away, for she cries out after us." But He answered and said, "I was not sent except to the lost sheep of the house of Israel." Then she came and worshiped Him, saying, "Lord, help me!" But He answered and said, "It is not good to take the children's bread and throw it to the little dogs." And she said, "Yes, Lord, yet even the little dogs eat the crumbs which fall from their masters' table." Then Jesus answered and said to her, "O woman, great is your faith! Let it be to you as you desire." And her daughter was healed from that very hour." (Matthew 15:21-28)

I'll be honest with you, the first time I read that passage, I couldn't believe Jesus would call a woman a *dog!* Man, try that today and be ready to duck! There is a lot here to unpack, but in light of our theme, *fishing for dogs,* let's not stray too far off our topic.

Back then the term *dog* simply meant non-Jew, or Gentile. Here, the Greek word *kunarion* meant puppy, or little harmless, helpless one. In other passages the word dog could and does imply vicious, impudent, or wild; but not here in Matthew 15.

This Canaanite woman knew her place in the society and culture of the day, but even as a little helpless dog she stood her ground knowing this Jesus of Nazareth could heal her daughter.

Jesus knew how to *fish for dogs* and was teaching His followers to do likewise.

Dogs are, in many ways like people. As a Pastor for nearly forty years, and a soul winner, I've learned fishing techniques.

I'm going to share a few stories as we move along in this little book. We will have some fun, and hopefully, you can learn how to catch dogs for the Kingdom of God!

" I think dogs are the most amazing creatures; they give unconditional love. For me, they are the role model for being alive."

– Gilda Radner

CHAPTER 1

DOGS, PEOPLE, AND GOD!

Why do we call dogs man's best friend? Where did that come from, or for that fact, where did dogs come from? Who was your favorite dog and why? I'm always talking to friends about why they choose a certain breed for a pet, or a hunting partner, or like a few of my friends, why show dogs.

HISTORY OF DOGS

Okay, where do these amazing creatures come from? The popular theory is all dogs come from ancient wolves. Now, there is no small debate about this. Naturalist, Mark Derr, says there are two main schools of thought.

Some researchers believe that humans domesticated wolves who were scrounging around their village for leftovers. Others believe that humans were taking care of wolf puppies over the years until they eventually evolved into dogs. Whatever! Most of us are glad we today have dogs and a large variety from which to choose.

One research institute using 14,000-year-old bones found in Siberia wrote, "Examining the animal's mitochondrial and nuclear DNA, and comparing them to genomes of modern wolves and dogs, the team summarized that there must have been a three-way-split among the species."

That's why we still have wild wolves and a variety of dogs. I, for one, am glad we have these wonderful pets for companionship, protection, aid, assistance, work, and play.

I have owned hunting dogs, watch dogs, lap dogs, stray dogs, purebred pedigree dogs, and mixed-breed mutts from the animal shelter, and loved them all (well, almost all).

Where did the popular saying, *dogs are man's best friend*, come from? This dates back thousands of years during the hunter-gatherer time when dogs were far more than pets. They were hunting helpers, protectors, providers, and at times, life-savers! Today we use the term watchdog.

It's not uncommon to see a sign on private property saying *Beware of Dog.* I saw one that said, "My dog's ok... beware of my mother-in-law." That's so wrong — but funny!

Today, we see dogs walking with their master, curling up on a couch next to their best friend, running around the park or beach fetching things, and having the time of their life.

Even though dogs share 99% of their DNA with wolves, dogs exude a sense of warmness towards other dogs (for the most part) and towards humans.

Who hasn't had one of those, *this is the worst day of my life,* days, yet, coming home to a grinning, wagging their tail, and licking your face furry friend seemed to melt away the cares of the day?

They love us no matter what. Forget to feed them, forget to leave enough water, scold them; it's ok, they bounce back instantly.

Today's dogs are also used in various professions as service dogs: military, police, drug sniffing, and seeing-eye dogs for the blind, plus many other callings.

As most of us know, dog spelled backward spells God. One

of my favorite personalities in the Old Testament is Caleb. His Hebrew name means *faithful like a dog*. Caleb was a very loyal, faithful solider/leader under Moses, and later Joshua. Faithful like a dog! I like that.

During my seventy-plus years on earth, I've owned dogs, shared dogs, and observed countless of my friends' dogs. Like people, they are all unique. This little book is their story!

FISHING

I have fished lakes, rivers, creeks, ponds, and even many of our oceans for trout, bass, salmon, tuna, sailfish, marlin, and sharks.

My choice of gear and bait depends on the particular appetite of the target. Fish, like people, have likes and dislikes when it comes to eating and, also like people, are somewhat predictable in their feeding hours. Take me for instance: I like an early, big breakfast, light lunch, and early sundown dinner.

I love fishing for trout in California's many lakes, east and northeast of San Jose up in the Sierra Mountains. The best time to catch trout is usually early in the morning when they are looking for food, or a couple of hours before dark. In my tackle box, or my son Adam's huge one, are an assortment of lures, worms, or my favorite power bait.

One morning, six of us were at one of our hot spot lakes up in the mountains, and I was the only one getting bites and catching trout. The others yelled, "Hey, Pastor, what color power bait are you using?" "Lime green power eggs," I answered.

Fish, like people, and yes, like dogs, can be funny and fickle. One day something looks appetizing, the next not so. Go figure! I often get a hankering for Chinese food, and I eat it three days in a row, then I won't eat it for a month or two.

One thing you learn fast if you're serious about fishing is you don't catch bass using trout bait (the good old-fashioned night crawler being the exception).

Salmon are extremely finicky, as are most of the oceans or rivers big species.

It's amazing how big of a lure a large mouth black bass will strike. One late afternoon I hooked a bass with a lure that was nearly as big as the fish!

My point in all this is, in soul winning, people are different, and it takes a variety of bait to lure them towards Christ.

My wife Carla is the best one-on-one soul winner I have ever seen, and this isn't a husband's exaggeration. She is as fearless and bold as they come. She likes to put it this way, "Honey, you throw the net, and I use a pole." In other words, I'm comfortable with crowds, and she prefers just one at a time.

SUMMARY

Dogs remind me of people and vice-versa. For over forty years, my wife and I have *fished for dogs.* Are you starting to get the itch to go fishing for dogs? Here's how... Keep turning the pages!

" **A dog can teach you unconditional love. If you have that in your life, things won't be too bad.**"

— Robert Wagner

CHAPTER 2

COCOA

The year was 1949. I was four, getting ready to enter kindergarten the coming fall. But as exciting as that was, it seemed like an eternity away.

It was still winter in Watsonville, California, just north of the Monterey – Carmel area. It was a stormy, rainy, very windy night, which was usual for our area so close to the Pacific Ocean.

I can't quite remember what my two sisters and I were doing, or if it was a weeknight or weekend. I think it was either a Friday or Saturday night. One of my sisters, Juanita, I believe, said, "Hey look, come here!"

Out on our small front porch was the cutest thing we ever saw. A little brown dog, soaked, shivering, and lost.

"Mom, come here, look!"

Our mother came out of the kitchen, and I remember her saying, "O poor thing, let him in."

That was the start of a twenty-four year long love affair with Cocoa, named for his color. We found out he was a short-haired Chihuahua (Chihuahua is named after a city in Mexico).

Our little Chihuahua was our overnight guest. Mom quickly threw a wet blanket over our excitement, "Kids, this precious little guy must belong to one of our neighbors. Tomorrow, go door-to-door and ask." (That's why I think it was a weekend).

Seems like early the next day, Judy and Juanita obeyed mom, hoping to high heaven he didn't belong to anyone but us. Our hope – maybe prayers – were answered. No one claimed him. Our neighborhood off Green Valley Road, next to Pinto Lake, was very small compared to today's standards, so it didn't take long for us to go skipping down Dick Phelps Avenue, named after my uncle Dick, with huge grins.

"Mom, can we keep him? He doesn't belong to anyone."

How could she say no to us three very happy kids? So, we named him Cocoa.

SUMMARY

Our house had a paned glass front door where real joy and life was visible even from the outside. Cocoa was attracted to the light. He saw people who didn't scare him, and even if he was a bit hesitant, he wanted in. He was cold, hungry, lonely, and desperate for love and acceptance.

It didn't take Cocoa long to fit right in as part of the family. Even years after we kids grew up, left home, and got married, Cocoa was always first our companion, and then Grandma and Grandpa's companion.

As a young man in my twenties who still had Sunday dinner with the family, it was always a treat to say, "Here Cocoa, come here boy."

He wasn't a spring chicken anymore; a bit wobbly with arthritis, nevertheless, here he would come, tail wagging, tongue out, ready for a big ol' dog kiss and love.

Over my nearly forty years of pastoring and helping people, I've encountered many people like Cocoa. Life can be a lonely, stormy, isolated experience. Some people seemingly don't belong to anyone, or anyplace. They are lost, scared, and desperate, but they see a lighthouse!

I wonder if our churches were as warm and welcoming as our home was way back in 1949, how many lost, hurting, lonely souls would take a peek inside and say, "I have found a home!"

" Be thou comforted little dog, thou too in the resurrection shall have a little golden tail.

– Martin Luther

CHAPTER 3

PATCHES

Patches, named after his coat of black patches on white fur, was one of those Heinz 57 dogs. In other words, I had no idea back in 1964 what breed he was, but he was the cutest mutt at the pound.

We don't use the term dog pound anymore. It's now Animal Care Center or Humane Society, or there's even one in my area called Care Companion Animal Rescue Effort. That's a mouthful.

Back in 1964, you could simply walk in, pick out your dog, throw down a couple of bucks, and have your new pet.

I wanted my son Adam, who was born in 1964, to grow up with a puppy, and Patches was perfect. A strange thing happened over the next year. Patches became very attached to Adam. Not to Adam's mom or me. Just Adam. He even slept in Adam's little room under his crib.

One day, after work, I wanted to see if my son was awake, and as I leaned over the railing of his crib, I heard this snarl. I peeked under the crib. Patches was baring his teeth, and he tried to bite me, but only got a grip on my pants cuff.

I yelled, "Patches! What's wrong with you!"

He had become Adam's guard dog and protector. He was truly man's best friend — just not mine. He was a bit more accommodating with Adam's mom, but Patches always watched her every move. He never grew out of his obsession to protect and to be close to little Adam.

Unfortunately, Patches never saw past his second birthday. He developed distemper, which I had never heard of, and he died.

Back then, dog pounds didn't automatically vaccinate for various diseases. They left it up to the new owner.

Because I was nineteen years old and had only one family dog, Cocoa, I didn't know the dog needed ongoing vaccinations for various dog maladies.

I cried over little Patches when I buried him. It was a family loss. Adam wondered what happened to him. It was hard to explain to an eighteen-month old that Patches was gone forever.

SUMMARY

How do we fish for people like Patches - people whose background is a mystery? People like Patches sometimes end up being taken at an early age to a foster home or orphanage. They often become people who are loners, who may have other issues, yet they need love and companionship. Perhaps they're needy, and they become extremely attached to one person they admire or look up to.

For example, there was a lady from our church who saw me as the dad she never had. After every service, she would hunt me down and wear me out with her story of the week. Even though it was irritating, especially after two services of pouring my heart out from the pulpit, I gave her time and space. I led her to Christ on her first visit, and I was stuck with her for years. She was like Patches, and I was her Adam. Like Patches, she later died way too young of cancer. Looking back, I'm glad I had both in my life.

" Dogs have given us
their absolute all.
We are the center
of their universe.
We are the focus
of their love, their
faith and trust.
They serve
us in return
for scraps."

– Roger A. Caras

CHAPTER 4

TROUBLE

My wife, Carla, and I were married way back in 1975, a week after Thanksgiving. As a wedding gift, a friend of ours gave us a unique gift – a puppy! He was a purebred Brittany Spaniel that came from a litter of an award-winning dog named Lance.

As a hunter, back in those days, I always loved watching Lance do his amazing thing. Brittany's are bird dogs. They have this God-given gift to sniff out game birds like pheasants, quail, and the such. They're called spaniels, but in reality, they are more akin to pointers or setters.

My friend, J.W., called him Trouble because even though he was the runt of the litter, he was the most aggressive when it came to nursing milk from his mother. I watched him go after a nipple many times, and even if one of his bigger brothers or sisters got there first, he would not be denied.

Carla and I laughed, but decided to keep the name – Trouble. We registered him with the American Kennel Association as *A Little Brit of Trouble*.

Once Trouble was weaned, we took him home and he instantly became family. He was a normal puppy, getting into everything and keeping us on our toes. When he was around six months old, I was playing with him out on our front lawn. A butterfly caught his attention as it slowly lit on a dandelion. He forgot about me and began stalking the butterfly, and as he got inches away, he went into a picture perfect three-point stance.

I yelled at Carla, who was in the kitchen, "Come here! Quick! Look at him!" I shouted with astonishment, "He's pointing like a real bird dog!" It lasted all of five seconds.

Once the butterfly took off, Trouble went back to being a puppy, running around the lawn with youthful enthusiasm.

Once Trouble got to be around ten months old, I began his training to prepare him for the next fall's hunting season. I followed the book, but he just didn't get it. He was more interested in playing than learning. With my long hours as an ironworker, I had little time and less patience to put the needed effort into his training, and I didn't have the resources to hire a professional trainer. So, little Trouble became the family pet.

October 1977 rolled around, and it was hunting season. All my buddies were excited, who, by the way, all had excellent bird dogs of various breeds.

The Friday night before opening day, J.W. called and asked, "Hey, Dick, you bringing little Trouble?"

I laughed and said, "No, J.W., he's not much interested in birds or hunting. He's Carla's sidekick and would rather hang out with her." J.W. responded, "Oh, come on, Dick. Bring him. I want to see the little guy. It will be good for him to reunite with Lance and see a couple of his brothers."

Carla, getting wind of my conversation, encouraged me to take him. "What can it hurt?"

That night, in my usual pre-hunt routine fashion, I laid out my gear on the rug in front of our fireplace: gun, shells, vest, hat, coffee thermos, and snacks. I set the alarm for 3 am – it was a two-hour drive down to the Woodland where we had leased our fields for pheasant and duck hunting.

When the alarm went off, I instantly sprang to my feet, excited for another opening day adventure with my buddies. As I left our bedroom and walked into our small but cozy front room, there was Trouble, laying on top of my shotgun, looking up at me, tail wagging.

Carla got up as well to wish me luck and say a prayer for safety, and I said, "Look at him. It's like he's saying, 'Where you go, I'll follow.'" Carla laughed and said, "He knows something is up, and he doesn't want to stay home."

Looking back, I wish I had had a camera handy. He was the cutest site. He was not going to be left behind. I grabbed some dog food and his water bowl, and off we went south down Highway 99 to join my friends.

Trouble slept the whole way until I made the turn onto a county road drawing close to our hunting grounds. Somehow, he sensed this would be a different day for him.

I spotted my friends' pickups, and as the sun began chasing away the dark, I could see dogs running around, stretching, and sniffing as dogs normally do.

I spotted J.W. and Lance, so I decided to pull in next to them. Trouble had not seen his dad since he was weaned at eight weeks. Trouble began trembling and whimpering with excitement peeking over the dash trying his best to take it all in.

I was not about to let him out because he had the bad habit of running off chasing whatever. More than once Carla and I had to get him from a neighbor, or we found him far away from our house. He didn't come when called, even if I yelled it at him. He lived up to his name, Trouble.

I parked, opened the door, and made sure he didn't escape! As I shut the door, he pressed his little nose up against the window with the most pitiful look of disappointment.

J.W. came over to say hi and asked, "Aren't you letting Trouble out?" "NO WAY!" I replied. "He will spot a jackrabbit and chase it all the way to Sacramento". J.W. laughed, "Okay!"

We hunted all morning with good results, nearly getting our limit of pheasants. It was lunchtime, and even though it was fall, it got hot. I was ready to call it a day and head home.

Watching Lance find and point pheasants was a beautiful thing. Lance was the best I'd ever seen. Even though I was one pheasant short, I was well-pleased with our first day's hunt.

J.W. said, "Hey, let's take Trouble for a walk and see what he can do." I laughed and said, "J.W., now I know why you got rid of him. He's useless out here, but Carla and I love him." J.W. said, "Oh, come on. He needs to stretch his legs and get a little exercise."

I was tired, but reluctantly agreed. I told J.W. he should put a leash on him in case he bolted. If I lost him, Carla would be furious with me.

J.W. grabbed a twenty-foot training leash, and we began walking back over the terrain we had already hunted hours earlier.

"Better grab your shotgun," J.W. said, "you never know." I laughed and said, "Sure," but I was secretly thinking, *Yes, I do know! This is nothing more than a midday stroll in the hot October sun.*

J.W. and I were casually talking about work, both being ironworkers for the same company, when J.W. said, "Dick! Look at Trouble!" Trouble had his nose to the ground, and he started working like an old pro.

"He's on a bird, Dick." J.W. was excited. I was amazed. "You sure?" "Look at him! Turn him loose, Dick!"

I unclipped the leash, and off he went, zigzagging on the scent of a pheasant. He came to a bush and made a picture perfect point.

"Better put a shell in your gun, Dick. He's got one." Dazed, I quickly shoved a shell into the chamber and slowly approached Trouble who was locked up in a three-legged point as you might see in a photo.

I kicked the bush, and a huge male pheasant flew out. I lowered my shotgun and brought him down.

Trouble took off, fetched the dead bird, brought him back to me, dropped him at my feet, and looked up for approval. My mouth was wide open in astonishment.

J.W. was laughing at me and said, "What did you expect, Dick? His father is a champion, and his father is in him. You only needed to get him to a place where he could do what he was born for."

SUMMARY

The right environment brought out Trouble's purpose in life – to hunt. Later in life, as I became a pastor and leader, I never forgot that day's lesson. If one is truly born-again, truly a child of God, and attends church on a regular basis, the Father of creation who lives in them will bring out the champion they are.

I've seen countless people struggle until they invited the Lord into their life, and then I watched them grow in God and find their purpose. It's a blessing I never tire of. Trouble was a bit of trouble until he was put in a place where he grew up and came alive.

" Dogs are wise.
They crawl away
into a quiet corner
and lick their
wounds and do not
rejoin the world
until they are
whole once more.

— Agatha Christie

CHAPTER 5

GEORGE

Of all the dogs I've had, or my family has had, the one I was the fondest of was George. We were in between dogs when my two youngest, Sarah and Jesse, began working their mom for a new one.

Dogs, as you all know, are a lot of work, so Carla was enjoying a bit of a respite from the feeding, caring, visits to the vet, and all the normal routines of being a dog owner/ provider. But the two kids knew how to work their mom – not unlike their ol' dad who grew up figuring out how to get my mom and Grandma to yield to my boyish charms.

So, one day while I was at the office, the three of them visited the local animal shelter to see what was available. A beautiful golden retriever immediately caught their eyes, but the shelter manager said, "Forget it. He's ruined. His previous owner who was a bad drunk has beaten the poor thing so often that he won't let anyone touch him.

We're putting him down tomorrow."

"No! Mom! We want him!" blurted out my two kids!

Carla's heart melted when she looked into his sad, scared, lonely eyes. "Okay, we will take him. Love and prayer will fix him!"

The manager gave her a look like, *good luck lady, but I bet you will bring him back.*

Now, I had no idea all this was playing out. I came home a bit late that day. It was late fall and already getting dark. As I walked into the house, I could tell something was up. Everyone had silly grins on their faces that prompted me to ask, "Okay, what's going on?"

"You tell him, mom," Sarah quickly answered, as she started walking slowly to the sliding door leading to our backyard.

"Now, what are you guys up to?" I fired back with a mixture of curiosity and more than a little anxiety.

As Carla pulled back the curtain, she said, "Look, honey, isn't he gorgeous?"

Lying against the side of our fence, with a frightened, bewildered look on his face was George. As I slid open the door, he jumped to his feet and growled.

"Honey, be careful." Carla went on to tell me his sad history and how he let her and the kids close, but he was terrified of men.

I sat down by the step several feet away and softly began talking to him. *Hello boy. It's okay. No one will hurt you.* After fifteen minutes or so, he slowly laid down, but he didn't take his eyes off me.

I went back in the house and got a piece of meat out of the fridge – chicken, I think – and I tossed it close to him. He lifted his eyes, looked at it, sniffed the air, and eventually inched over to it, snatched it, and darted back to his safe place.

"Good boy," I said, as I slowly got up and went inside. "Let's leave him alone and see if he gets used to his new home."

The next night I repeated the routine, but this time threw a piece of meat a little closer to me than him. After he thought about it for quite a while, he slowly approached it, grabbed it quickly, and ran back to his comfort zone.

Night after night we did this, and I constantly reassured him in a soft, slow voice, *It's okay boy. I'm your friend.*

Then came the big night. I took a nice piece of leftover steak and held it in my hand. By then we were calling him

George. "Here George, come and get it. You're going to love this."

George couldn't resist, so he came very slowly, and again, without taking his eyes off me, eased up to my offering. This time I held onto his dinner with my right hand, and ever so slowly lifted my left hand to his head and patted him gently, talking all the while. *Good boy, George. Good boy.*

I let the steak go and instead of running back to his now favorite resting spot, he stayed and laid down next to me and let me pet him and comfort him. Once he finished his treat, he licked my hand and gave me a look I will never forget. A look of *thank you, I'm home!*

From that day on, George was part of the family. He was happy as can be. Everyone who visited loved George, especially our kids' friends.

Golden Retrievers usually love water, but not George. We had a small pool in our backyard. Summers here can get above ninety degrees and my kids and their friends lived in that pool. George would run around, barking at them, tail wagging, having a great time, but none of us could coax George into the pool. Once in a while, he would stick a paw onto the first step, but that was it.

The kids began calling him *Chicken George.*

Looking back, I think George loved Carla more than all of us, because she took more time caring for him than the rest of us.

One day the kids got the idea to act like they were drowning. They got into the pool in their usual fashion, and of course, George was all excited, running around the edges, barking at them in his playful style.

Then they went into their act, "Help, George, help!" They waved their arms and slapped the water frantically, went under, and begged George to save them.

George didn't know what to do. He was running around in circles, now barking in a different tone, tail not wagging in dog-joy, but frantic and alarmed. Finally, he jumped into the deep end and did his best to rescue them. It became a daily routine with us all.

From that day on he was a pool-loving dog. We couldn't get him out of the water! He had found paradise, especially in those hot summer days.

The kids' favorite pool game became *Save me, George.* The following Thanksgiving, that fun, silly, pool game would save a life.

Thanksgiving at our house was, and still is, a big family and friends food-o-rama. Carla goes all out, and boy are we glad!

Carla's sister, Karen, who lived nearby, was at our house with her family. Karen had twins a couple of years earlier, Joshua and Jordan — two cute little blonde kids. Jordan, the quiet, shy type, and Joshua, the talkative, extrovert who was always exploring.

Our neighbors across the street and down half a block were owners of a pit bull. That afternoon, being a chilly fall day, we were all in the house, the guys watching football and the girls cooking.

Joshua had slipped out of the house, and for some reason ended up in our front yard. He was barely three at the time if my memory serves me well. Somehow the neighbors pit bull got loose from his cage and ended up at our house.

By God's grace, Caleb, Joshua's older brother peeked out of the window and saw the pit bull stalking Joshua. Joshua loved dogs and thought it was a nice doggie to pet.

The pit bull attacked and had Joshua's head in his death grip. When George heard the commotion, he ran and jumped the pit bull. The attacking dog let go of Joshua and turned his attention to George, and the fight was on.

By then, Caleb had alerted us. I grabbed a golf club and ran out and wacked the rib cage of the big pit bull before he killed George. He let George go then turned towards me growling, but I stared him down. He saw I was not scared and he ran back home.

We rushed Joshua to the hospital where they sewed up his wounds. The police came and took the pit bull away to be put down. The police told us a week before a child in our town was killed by a pit bull in a similar situation.

Once Joshua got sewed up and had a shot or two for infection, Carla and Karen began saying, "Praise you, Jesus, for saving Joshua." Little Joshua piped up in his cute voice, "Praise George, he saved me!" Everyone laughed. Thank you, Lord, and yes, thank you, George.

SUMMARY

During my nearly forty years of pastoring, I've seen people, like George, who've been abused, beaten, and given up on. Yet, once they found God, God's people, and a safe church, they came out of their pain and blossomed into courageous, confident, never afraid of no devil or anyone's opinion of them people, and came into the awareness that they have a purpose here on earth.

George taught me a great lesson. Be very patient and kind with hurting people, for it reaps wonderful benefits.

" A dog barks when his master is attacked. I would be a coward if I saw that God's truth is attacked and yet would remain silent.

— John Calvin

CHAPTER 6

J.T.

Loving Brittany Spaniels, and missing our first one, Trouble, Carla and I decided to find us another one. As I said already, brits are a breed of gun dog, primarily used for bird hunting (pheasant, chukar, quail, etc.)

Carla found J.T. and named him *Jubilee Triumph*. Unlike Trouble, who was smallish, even for a brit, J.T. was long-legged and lean. He was also super fast, and he loved to show it. When we had him, we lived in Morgan Hill, California, just south of San Jose, and we had plenty of room for pets. Our two-acre mini-ranch was ideal for a hyperactive dog like J.T.

I fenced off a little over an acre with chicken wire nailed to an existing wooden fence so I wouldn't have to keep J.T. on a chain. I thought five feet high of chicken wire secured and sturdy would be plenty safe.

Little did I know J.T. was a climber! The first time he

escaped he was gone for three days. I finally got a call from a man a mile away who found him thanks to the nametag on his collar. He was hungry and tired.

When I went to retrieve my run away retriever, J.T. didn't seem excited to see me. In fact, he acted like he wanted to stay with the elderly man, who I learned was a widower. I felt bad putting J.T. in my truck after I saw the disappointment on the man's face. I think they bonded in their short time together.

Well, back at the ranch, I decided to see just how Houdini pulled off this amazing feat. I turned him loose in the fenced-off area, then I hid. It didn't take ten minutes before he started climbing like a professional rock climber.

I jumped up from my hiding spot and yelled, "J.T.!"

Dogs, I'm told, have every human emotion, and fear of being in trouble is one of them. J.T. climbed down and took off for the other end of the fence and stared back at me, probably wondering what form of punishment I would administer.

I gave him a couple of loud bad dog scoldings, to let him know I was very unhappy with my Papillon escape artist.

So, I came to the conclusion that the only option would

be to build a fully-enclosed dog run to limit his ability to go exploring. One Saturday someone left the dog gate unlocked and, yep, he figured out how to open it, and off to the races he went.

Once again I got a call. This time it was a nice lady who lived a few miles away. I got in my truck with my son Jesse, shaking my head in frustration, and off we went to fetch J.T.

As we drove up to the modest but very nice home, we saw bikes and toys in the yard. We knocked, and a young boy answered and invited us in. There was J.T., playing with three kids, wagging his tail, licking their faces, and ignoring me.

He glanced up at me with one of those *Oh, you* looks, with little interest.

"C'mon, J.T.," I said, as I put the leash on his collar. The nice lady had explained to her kids that J.T. didn't belong to them. The look of disappointment on their faces got to me, but J.T. was our dog... I thought.

A few months later, J.T. got out again – don't ask me how! It was a Saturday – I was up at the church getting ready for Sunday morning. There was a knock at the door. J.T. got run over by a car right in front of our house. It crushed his lower back and legs.

Carla put him in her car and started praying for him as she quickly drove to our local veterinarian. The prognosis was not good. The choice was to spend thousands of dollars, with no guarantee of success, or put him to sleep, which was the vet's suggestion. Carla thanked him and took him home. She took out her anointing oil, smeared it all over him, praying to God for a real *doggone miracle.*

This may seem hard to believe, but days later, J.T. was running around like a deer. Was the vet wrong? No, he X-rayed J.T. The x-rays showed the extent of the damage.

Later, I preached a message about God loving animals, especially the ones we love.

Well, it doesn't end there. J.T. had one more great escape. I actually hoped I wouldn't get a call this time. A month or so after his last escape, I was in downtown Morgan Hill. I saw a green Ford pickup with an elderly gentleman driving. Yep, there he was, J.T., with his head hanging out the passenger window, sniffing the air, pleased as punch.

At first, I was going to follow him and ask him to pull over, but I slowed down and watched the man and J.T. disappear in the distance. I pulled over and said, "J.T., I hope you have found a home where you're happy and content".

SUMMARY

There are people like J.T. who have a bit of a wanderlust nature. They're never quite ready to settle down, and always looking for the new, the exciting, the adventure called *next*. In my nearly forty years of pastoring, I have seen more than I can count of people like J.T.

I've led them to Christ, loved them, helped heal old wounds and hurts, fellowshipped with them, even had them in my home for a summer BBQ, then all of a sudden they disappear! Gone!

I'd ask around the church, "Hey, have you seen so-n-so or their family?"

"Oh, I hear they're over at the such-n-such church; or, I think they moved out of the area."

Some people come, and some people go, but my job is to preach Jesus to them while they're in my care even if they suit up and climb the fence, so-to-speak. I bless them and thank God that I had a season with them.

" It's not the size of the dog in the fight, it's the size of the fight in the dog.

– Mark Twain

CHAPTER 7

OL' BLUE

In this little book, I'm writing about dogs I've owned and dogs I've known. I grew up hunt-ing and fishing, and even though my hunting days are minimal, I still get a kick out of fishing, especially with my two sons and our friends.

Blue was a pit pull – a trained wild boar dog Where I live now, in the foothills of East San Jose, up against the Mount Hamilton range, we have a problem with wild pigs. Their num-bers over the past twenty years have escalated to the point the county began issuing special permits to harvest them in order to reduce their numbers. They were tearing up lawns, parks, and even the nearby golf course.

During the dry, summer months, they come down from the hills to root and dig up food from watered areas, like my front lawn. It's very costly to replace grass, so when I got the chance to harvest one or two, I said yes.

Ed, my brother-in-law, my son, Jesse, who was fourteen, and I met our guide, Sam and his buddy, Joe. They were a couple of good ol' boys that looked like they had just stepped out of a Zane Grey novel.

In the back of their pick-up truck were four cages with two hounds and two pit bulls.

I had never hunted for pigs before, so I asked, "How are we going about this today?"

It was about five in the morning, and as we sipped on hot coffee, Sam and Joe explained our strategy. The hounds would pick up the scent of the pigs, and once we got on a hot trail the pits would be turned loose to corner the target hog, and that's when I would have my chance.

Sam, while introducing us to the dogs, said: "Well, this might be Ole Blue's last hunt."

I could see Blue was scarred from many battles with big, fierce, dangerous pigs, and he limped from arthritis and old injuries. Blue was around twelve which was up there in years for his breed and his very dicey profession.

Well, to leave out the bloody details, I got my 300-pound boar, and as Sam and Joe began to field dress our harvest,

Sam asked if Jesse and I could walk Ol' Blue back to the truck and let him rest in his cage.

"Hey Pastor, please give him water but no food, ok?" "Sure Sam, see you when you're done," I answered.

We had to walk slow for Ol' Blue was spent. He was so tired, Jesse and I had to pick him up and put him in his portable doghouse. Once we put a pan of water in with him, we closed the door, and as Sam told us, we padlocked it.

Then, Jesse and I fell fast asleep. We were as tired as Ol' Blue. The cab of Sam's truck felt like the Ritz Hotel!

Ed stayed with Sam and Joe, watching the process and the anticipation of a Hawaiian-style roasted wild pig luau! Ed was quite the cook.

As I snoozed away, I kept hearing this crunching sound. I woke Jesse up, "You hear that?" I rolled the window down looking out and up in the trees. "What is that?"

Just then, bang, wham! Ol' Blue had chewed through the wood frame door, knocked it open, and bolted out the back of Sam's truck.

Jesse and I jumped out, calling after him to no avail. He was gone in less than sixty seconds.

"Oh boy, Jesse, Sam is going to be upset," I said, as I looked at the damage to his portable kennel. I couldn't believe a dog could chew open a locked door.

After an hour or so I could hear voices coming up out of a hollow. There was Ol' Blue leading the way with the other three dogs following, and Sam, Joe and Ed bringing a dead pig wrapped up in cheese cloth and gunny sack.

"Hey, Sam, man I'm sorry Ol' Blue got out." Sam laughed, "Oh, Pastor, it's the third time he's chewed through his door." What he then said I'll never forget. "Blue isn't satisfied until he sees the pig in the truck. He doesn't trust us that we will complete the job."

He came down to make sure his pig was coming back to his truck.

Ol' Blue died a few months later. I was sad, but glad I got to hunt with him on his last hunt.

Ed, my brother-in-law, was also on his last hunt. Ed was eaten up with cancer, and I was surprised that he wanted to go on such an arduous adventure, which took a lot out of Jesse and me, but he insisted.

Ed passed away not long after Ol' Blue.

SUMMARY

Ed, like Blue, was a tough ol' dog. Ed had a hard upbringing, lived hard, drank hard, cussed with the best of them, wreaked havoc in his marriage to my sister Juanita, but I had the opportunity to lead him to Christ.

Ed's last job was helping me design and build our current sanctuary. Even while being in unbelievable pain, he wanted to see the job completed. I've met a lot of *Eds*. Elderly people who still have something to add to the Kingdom. His wisdom and encouragement to me during hard times will always be remembered.

If you're reading this book, and you're up there in years, remember some of the Bible's greatest heroes were senior citizens just waiting to get out of their cage!

"You want a friend in Washington, D.C.? Get a dog."
– Harry S. Truman

CHAPTER 8

MAC

Kurt was a duck-hunting buddy who had a male Black Labrador named Mac. If memory serves me well, he named Mac after his uncle who loved to hunt ducks.

Kurt would joke, saying, "If Mac sees someone walking down the street in camo gear with a shotgun slung over his shoulder, he's gone." Mac had one thing on his mind: *get me where I can have fun and do my thing.*

One winter a group of us went on a trip up North close to the Oregon border to a famous hunting area called Tule Lake. It was colder than usual, and it even snowed a bit. Even though we dressed for inclement weather, it was brutal. I was miserable, and as much as I loved hunting, I was ready to get back to our camp and build a fire.

However, Mac, who was getting up there in years, was

ready to go in spite of the weather. He would get this look of excitement and expectation on his face. I said, "Hey, Mac, aren't you freezing?" He ignored me and kept watching the sky for ducks and maybe a goose or two. It was so cold the lake had pockets of ice in places an inch thick, and it also had started snowing.

I kept thinking about my warm sleeping bag back at camp, yet we toughed it out. The ducks came in that day, and we limited-out in a couple of hours. The last mallard to come down was dropped by Kurt, Mac's owner.

The bird glided quite a way off and eventually came down in a huge Tule patch.

Kurt said, "Too bad, too far away. Let's head in." But Mac would have nothing to do with that. He leaped out of the boat, broke through the ice and started swimming towards the target.

Kurt yelled, "Mac, come back boy!" but to no avail. Kurt knew looking for that duck would be like looking for a needle in a haystack. He shrugged his shoulders and added, "Well, if he doesn't make it, he died doing what he loved the most." I encouraged him saying, "Let's wait and see. He's a tough old dog."

An hour had passed, and our hope was fading fast, plus, fog had set in making matters worse.

We called out, "Here Mac. Over here boy." Nothing but eerie silence... Then we heard ice breaking, snorting, and huffing sounds off in the fog. Yep, here came Mac with the duck in his mouth, nearly half dead from the cold. He was also bleeding from cuts he got as he broke through the ice.

We had to help him into the boat. He was spent! Kurt laughed out loud, with tears in his eyes, patting Mac with pride and relief.

Ol' Mac slept all the way back to camp and a big part of the next day.

Some dogs you never forget.

SUMMARY

There are people, like Mac, who have hobbies and interests that are very important to them. I have found that friendship evangelism is the most productive way to establish trust and a relationship around felt needs. I've gotten golf junkies to come to church after playing many a round with them while never talking religion or church; just being their friend. Once they find out there is a rhythm to life where there's room for God, golf, family, work, and other things, it's not hard to catch these dogs.

" **Once you have had a wonderful dog, a life without one, is a life diminished.**

— Dean Koontz

CHAPTER 9

ZEUS
"THE MIRACLE DOG"

I've been telling stories of dogs I've owned, and dogs I've known. However, an article in People Magazine (August 18, 2015) touched me. Let me share the highlights.

Ben, a Chief Warrant Officer in the Military, got transferred to South Korea, and his family was not able to bring their beloved Zeus, a Rottweiler mix, with them. So, Ben and his wife, Melody, decided to place Zeus in the care of friends in North Carolina where Ben was stationed. Tough decision!

Ben and Melody got regular updates from their friends on how Zeus was doing. Unfortunately, several months after their stay in Seoul, they received devastating news that Zeus had died. Those of us who have had a beloved pet die unexpectedly can relate to the pain.

Years passed, and Ben and his family finally returned to the U.S. settling in the state of Washington. One day they got the shock of their lives. Out of the blue, they received a phone call from a pet hospital in North Carolina saying that Zeus was very much alive. He was found wandering the streets and woods of Raleigh as a stray. Someone befriended him and brought the poor thing to the pet hospital.

Thankfully years earlier, Ben had a microchip implanted in Zeus with information that allowed the hospital to track him down. Zeus, like Lazarus, returned from the dead!

One can only imagine what went through Ben and Melody's mind and heart. Let's bring him home.

There was a slight problem. Zeus had heartworms, which is curable, but takes time, so Zeus was unable to fly.

But wait! Here comes a good samaritan, Rachel, a manager at the Banefield Pet Hospital, who agreed to drive Zeus 3,000 miles to be reunited with his family who lived in the state of Washington.

This story would make a good movie! It's a doggone good one.

SUMMARY

People can get lost in life. Change can throw some people into a downward spiral. Families can be torn apart by addictions, loss of jobs, relationships, and even one's health. Every day I see people sleeping under overpasses, wandering the streets, or begging for money. I often wonder what happened – what event or twist of fate got them into their desperate, sad situation? But, thanks to God, there are caring, good samaritans in this world who love those whom God loves.

In our story, one picked up Zeus and brought him to a place of care and healing! The other good samaritan drove him home to Ben and Melody.

Every Sunday, as I turn onto our street leading to our church, I usually stop and say *hi* to Bill. Bill is a Vietnam Vet who is homeless, and he panhandles every Sunday rain or shine. I always stop to put a few bucks into his hand.

One Sunday, Bill said, "Hey Pastor, I need to hear you preach today. I'm not doing well physically."

Ben and Melody Harworth reunited with Zeus.

Banfield Pet Hospital in Raleigh, North Carolina.

"I'm on it, Bill." I knew he needed to stay at his corner to get a few handouts, so I told my assistant Isaac, "Hey, go fetch Ol' Bill and bring him to sit with Carla and me."

I introduced Bill to the early service as my friend. Now, one of our good samaritans picks him up each week. You can actually see the change in him. He's loved, accepted, and honored as a Veteran of our great country.

If you get a chance – look for a Zeus or an Ol' Bill, they're out there!

" **Heaven goes by favor. If it went by merit, you would stay out and your dog would go in.**

— Mark Twain

CHAPTER 10

PACO

Paco was a 120-pound Chesapeake Bay Retriever of the sporting breed groups. They are known for their protective, and also very affectionate, behavior.

Paco, like his owner, Big Ed, was unique. Ed was 400-pounds, 6'4" and, like Paco, he was bigger than life. Both were extremely intimidating to just look at, but both were huge teddy bears. I was not going to write about Paco and Ed because both recently died tragically. Their ashes were buried together in a nearby Military Cemetery.

A few years ago, Paco, in the prime of his life, got cancer and slowly and sadly we all watched him lose weight and eventually his young, happy life. It tore Ed's heart out and grieved many of us who loved Paco.

Not long after, Big Ed was killed in a small plane crash in Reno, Nevada. Ed was family! His funeral was one of the hardest I have ever conducted.

Ed was in the Army Special Forces, and he fought in Panama in the early nineties. He survived snakebites, a helicopter crash, and other close calls. Later, after his time in the Army was over, he became a bounty hunter, a private investigator, and a bail bondsman. That's what he was doing in Reno when on his way back, he and two others were tragically killed at the airport after an ill-fated takeoff.

When I first met Ed, it took a while for him to warm up to me because he found out I'm a pastor.

We met on a golf course during a match set-up by a mutual friend, who was also named Ed, who didn't tell Big Ed I was a preacher.

Ed had a real bad childhood experience in a super strict church where his mom was taught that everything fun was evil. Ed and his sister suffered so much verbal and physical abuse that once they were old enough, they swore to never set foot in a church ever again.

With my ironworker, biker, rodeo rookie background, Ed eventually warmed up to me, and we became close. He even started coming to church to hear me speak. However, his crazy hours chasing runaways who jumped bail or bailing someone out who got into a Saturday night problem greatly reduced Ed's church attendance.

When he got Paco as a pup, it was obvious they were two peas in a pod. Ed was single, and he took Paco everywhere. Eventually, Ed got Paco a friend, Jillie! Jillie was a female Black Lab, and the two became best friends.

Paco, like Ed, had a hard time being alone. If Ed had to be gone, chasing down a bail jumper (someone who ran out on a court appearance), Paco, even though he had Jillie, would get so stressed out missing Ed that he would chew up anything that was chewable – furniture, rugs, towels, boots, suits, and other things. I know, because I witnessed the carnage first-hand. I've never before seen such damage done by one dog!

Paco was so connected to Ed that Ed being gone too long would traumatize him. It's called separation anxiety. I'm not sure how many thousands of dollars Ed lost because of Paco's stress, but imagine it was a multiple of thousands.

Most would probably just get rid of a dog like Paco, but not Ed. Paco was, in a way, like the son Ed never had. When Paco was diagnosed with cancer, Ed went into an emotional funk. It was hard for us to see him hurting over his buddy, Paco.

Just writing this makes me tear up a bit because I miss them both. He told a friend, also a vet from the

Vietnam War, "If I go before you, bury my ashes with Paco."

RIP Ed and your Beloved Paco.

SUMMARY

Fishing for Paco people is an exercise in patience. It took a while for Ed to warm up to me and discover that I wasn't some hyper-religious nut case with a bible in one hand and a club in the other.

Likewise, it took a while for Paco to warm up to me. Boy, once he did, he tried to be a lapdog. His sloppy kisses were gross, yet hilarious. More than once his slobber would send a nice coat or sweater off to the cleaners. Carla and I would often bring steak scraps for him and Jillie, or other tasty treats. He loved it when he spotted our car pulling up in the driveway.

The world is full of Paco people. They march to the beat of a different drummer, but they are precious to God.

This I know… Ed is in Heaven with Jesus and maybe, just maybe, with Paco too!

" Ever consider what our dogs must think of us? I mean, here we come back from a grocery store with the most amazing haul, chicken, pork, half a cow. They must think we're the greatest hunters on earth.

— Anne Tyler

CHAPTER 11

CANE CORSOS

I went to visit a pastor friend, Rick, in San Antonio, years back, at his ranch in the Hill Country, several miles from the city. His house sits back a few hundred yards off a country road, and as my driver made the turn, I spotted two huge dogs coming down the driveway to see who we were. The closer they got, the less sure I was that I wanted to exit my driver's truck. They looked like big Pit Bulls or Rottweilers, but I couldn't tell.

My driver, Pastor Gary, noticed my uncertainty and laughed, "Ah, that's just Maya and Sadie. They're great dogs, and gentle."

I joked a bit and answered, "Well, Pastor, prove it! You get out first." I wasn't 100% sure it was as safe as Gary said.

Well, sure enough, as Gary said, here they came, tails wagging, running around, sniffing and licking while slobbering all over Gary who didn't seem to mind. Then they spotted me, and it was my turn to be introduced to a breed I never heard of, Cane Corsos.

Pastor Rick was up on the porch waiting for us, and as he walked towards us he yelled, "Okay enough. Go lay down."

The two Corsos instantly obeyed, although reluctantly. It wasn't every day they had new friends to play with.

After shaking hands and sitting out on Rick's porch for a while in the heat of the day, I asked Rick about his dogs. His affection and love was instantly obvious. He sounded like he was describing one of his kids to Gary and me. Gary had visited the ranch a time or two before, but it had been awhile.

Rick explained how he was first introduced to this breed, and instantly took a liking to them. Cane Corso is an Italian name and an Italian breed known for their even temperament, their calm and stable personality, and their trainability.

Rick said they are some of the smartest dogs anywhere. They are great companions, and in Italy, they are used as guard dogs. Rick went on to say how good they are with his grandkids who ride them like horses and pull their ears as kids will do, yet his Corsos love the attention, albeit a bit abusive.

Over my many visits through the years, I have become very fond of Rick's dogs. Maya is now fourteen. She moves slowly, and she's a bit gray around her face, but she still comes to greet me when I pay Rick a visit.

SUMMARY

There are people who, at first look are intimidating, even dangerous, yet if allowed to get close enough to share Christ, reveal an amazingly soft heart even though they exhibit a rough exterior.

I've been around bikers from various motorcycle clubs since the early sixties, even some of the most notorious clubs. I've been privileged to lead many to Christ, marry them, fellowship with them, and at times, bury them. Once the bond of trust was formed, I had a friend for life.

Don't be afraid of the Cane Corsos of this world. They too need Jesus!

" **Dogs are not our whole life,
but they make our lives whole.**

— Roger Caras

~

CHAPTER 12

THE COMFORTER

Recently I was at a birthday party for a pastor friend in Texas. I spoke at his church on Sunday, and that night, folks, family, and church leaders met at his house for a BBQ.

He introduced me to a lady who was a true dog lover. She had five dogs and was looking for more. I told her about this little book I was in the process of writing.

What I didn't know was her boyfriend had died just a month prior to that evening. I gave my condolences and told her my wife and I would pray for her.

She then told me of her favorite dog of the five that seemed to pick up on her sadness and wouldn't leave her side. He even started jumping up on the bed at night and snuggling up to her. She said it was like he knew and wanted her to know he felt her loss.

I forgot the exact breed, but it was a small mixed breed.

She opened up about her *bad luck* with men and ex-mates. She laughed and said, "Well, one thing about my dogs, they will never hurt me or abuse me."

She reminded me somewhat of my sister Judy who, like her, had poor luck with men. Her little mutt, Jiggs, is now her constant companion. She even brings Jiggs to the office, and I have to be careful that I don't step on him. His devotion to her is evident. He's not overly friendly with any of us, only Judy.

SUMMARY

There are really good people out there, in this world of ours, who form strong bonds with a spouse, kids, or a best friend. People can only fill a part of the heart's need. I'm convinced God planned it that way, that no matter how in love we are, or fond of someone, only God can make us complete.

The challenge is convincing good, honest, hard-working people, who are for the most part happy, yet without God, that they need God. Like the rich young ruler who thought it was all good, but Jesus showed him it wasn't! So, we continue to pray for everyone.

" **Some of my best leading men have been dogs and horses.**

– Elizabeth Taylor

CHAPTER 13

A DOG NAMED MONEY

By Larry Huggins

I asked my long time friend of more than thirty years, who is also an associate minister here at our church, Jubilee, to write about his favorite dog. Here's an incredible story of his dog, Money, that I think you'll enjoy.

MONEY...

You'll love this. Picture me outside, hollering, "Hereee Money! Come Moneeey! Money come!"

Charging towards me, in soft light, slow motion, with a classical sound track comes the most beautiful dog you've ever seen – a dog named, Money.

Money was our blond, blue-eyed, Doberman Pincher. No, he wasn't albino. The American Doberman Association recognizes five colors of Doberman: black and tan, red, fawn, blue, and blond. Our dog was a creamy, ivory color with a white shield.

The developer of the Doberman Pincher breed, a Nineteenth Century, German, dogcatcher, named Herr Karl Doberman, wanted to produce a dog with the perfect combination of strength, loyalty, intelligence, and ferocity. I believe he succeeded.

Money was our once-in-a-lifetime dog. He was the smartest, bravest, most obedient, beautiful, and delightful dog I've ever known.

We picked him from the litter because he was, without a doubt, the alpha male. We wanted an intact, alpha male for protection because we lived in Mexico, and we drove thousands of miles on the highways and back roads.

At first, my wife, Loretta, wasn't sure she could handle a ninety-five pound, alpha Doberman. I said, "You'll learn to be the alpha female, and you'll keep him in check." She did, and she handled him beautifully. When I was away, she felt safe inside our large, high-walled, Mexican compound with Money guarding her.

The trainers at the world famous Triple Crown Dog Academy said Money was the smartest dog they'd ever known. Triple Crown is a 480-acre, state-of-the-art operation that trains thousands of field dogs, show dogs, and service dogs from around the world. They know dogs.

Money loved the rigorous training regimen. He went through multiple levels of obedience training, protection training, and agility training. He loved being challenged, and he excelled at everything.

He was a rock-star at Triple Crown. Every time he came on the property the employees would spread the word with their walky-talkies, "Money's coming!" Then a dozen or more employees would muster outside, waiting for him to bound out of our SUV, prance around, and pose for the Paparazzi.

His trainers claimed that he was the most vocal dog they'd ever met. I believe it. He had a huge vocabulary. It wouldn't have surprised me if he had said, "Morning Pa. What are we doing today?"

He barked like a German shepherd, bayed like a coonhound, yelped like a coyote, and howled like a wolf, and he made hundreds of other sounds I'd never heard a dog make.

He pointed like an Irish setter, tracked like a bloodhound, and fought like a Pit Bull. I think I've seen and heard the traits of every dog Herr Doberman used in his amazing breed.

He wouldn't like this, but at times his movements were almost feline – like a panther.

Most dogs at Triple Crown were boarded in kennels. Not Money. His trainers competed for the chance to have him sleep in their homes at night. However, it was our attention he craved. His trainers said, "We know you treat Money well because he gets so excited when he knows you're coming to get him."

We called him our Velcro dog because he had to be in constant contact with us, even when we walked. The exception was when he went for his daily run. That's when the greyhound in him came out.

What a runner! He was poetry in motion, and fast – real fast. One day, some kids stopped playing and just stared at him. One of them said, "Gee, that dog can run!"

He had five gaits. He walked, trotted, pranced, cantered, galloped, and ran like Secretariat at the Derby. Sometimes I ran with him, and he would lope beside me without effort. I would pick up the pace, and he would think, "It's on!" Off he would go in a flash. No catching him.

He loved car trips. We often loaded our big, black, Ford Expedition the day before we left. Money's crate would be in the back, near the cargo door. To make sure we wouldn't leave without him, he would jump in the crate and refuse to get out of the truck. I would say, "Ok, but you're going to be here all night. We're going to bed." About an hour later he would sheepishly come into the house and flop down on his bed and groan.

The next morning he would wake me with the slap of his big paw. "Time to go."

On Mexican road trips, military roadblocks always stopped us. The young soldiers would ask me to open the rear hatch on the truck. I always said, "Ok, but be careful. I have a dog in the back." When Money saw the Federales he would go into protection mode – baring his teeth, barking, and biting the bars on his cage. He seemed ferocious.

The soldiers would freeze. I would say, "Let me talk to

him." Then, in Spanish, I would say, "Calmate, ellos son amigos (Calm down, these are friends)."

Money would settle down, and I would slowly open his crate. I'd tell the wary soldiers, "Go ahead. You can pet him." Someone would timidly touch him, and then they all would take turns petting him (which Money loved), and then everyone would laugh and smile. Without fail, one of the soldiers would start talking about his favorite, childhood dog, and we would all bond in our mutual love of dogs. Then, we would shake hands, like old friends, and they would wave us through the checkpoint without searching our SUV.

The same thing happened at the border with the U.S. Customs and Immigration. Money was our ambassador of good will.

I realized money was super smart when he was just a pup. I taught him to take me by the hand and lead me to the back door if he needed to do his business. He learned on the first try. But that's not why I thought he was extraordinary.

One day, soon after he learned the potty trick, he wanted my attention, but I was watching TV, and I didn't want to play. So, he devised a little scheme. He went into the laundry and came out with one of my wife's athletic socks, trying to entice me into a game of keep away. I said, "No way. Gimme that sock."

He reluctantly dropped it into my hand. I stuck it under my leg and went back to watching my program. Money poked around and tried to get the sock. But I said, "No, you're not getting this sock."

(Remember, he was just a puppy. His ears and tail hadn't even been docked).

He walked away, paused, and then he circled back and took my hand in his mouth and pulled me towards the door. I said, "Oh, you've got to potty." When we got to the door, I opened it. But instead of going outside, he ran back to my chair and grabbed the sock.

I said, "Uh oh, you rascal. I'm going to have to keep my eye on you."

One evening we left him outside for a couple of hours, and he broke *into* the house. When we got home, he met us at the door. "Welcome home, Pa."

Here's another of his self-taught tricks. There was a wrought iron gate between the backyard and the front yard. It was secured with a hasp and a dead bolt. He figured out how to stick his nose through the bars, lift the hatch, slide it to the side, and kick the gate open. One, two, three – free!

Things like that kept us on our toes.

He was also the bravest dog we'd ever seen. He never backed down from any threat. Once, he got into a fight with a military trained, Great Dane, attack dog. He would have destroyed the larger dog if we hadn't taken control of him.

But there was a soft side to him, too. We called him our hippie dog. He would stroll through fields of bluebonnets and sniff flowers. Once, a butterfly landed on his nose. Another time, we found him whimpering over a dead bird he had found in a field of wildflowers.

There were times he and I would play-fight for hours. I would let him get rough with me and I would be rough with him. Afterward, all ninety-five pounds of him would slowly climb into my lap and curl up. He needed to be held.

All his alpha bravado vanished when we visited the veterinarian clinic. "You're going to put that thermometer where?" He kept his tail tucked, and cowered behind me, trembling. He had some bad experiences with the vet.

We learned a lot about dogs when we put him through graduate school. Dogs have a keen sense of fairness, and they want to be treated with respect. The only time he defied us was a time when we unintentionally treated him unfairly. He snarled at us. However, we realized he was right and we were wrong. Thank God, he was quick to forgive. We immediately kissed and made up. "Aw, shucks. It's ok, Pa."

As the dog whisperer, Cesar Millan, often says, "I do more to train dog owners than I do dogs."

Double-minded people drive their dogs crazy. Dogs understand rules and boundaries. There's no gray area in their thinking. They get confused when the rules are arbitrarily changed, or the boundaries are moved.

For example, we make a rule: "No getting on the furniture." A boundary is set between the floor and the furniture.

The dog's okay with that — the floor is his space, the sofa is our space.

One day, we're lonely, so we say, "C'mon Puppy. Get up here and keep me company."

He thinks, "Oh boy, the rules have changed." So, he jumps on the couch and enjoys being petted. "Hmm, this is nice."

The next day, he jumps on the sofa, and we yell, "Bad dog! Get off the couch." Then, he gets smacked. He thinks, "My humans are nuts."

Now, the dog's angry and confused, and he distrusts us. His masters are unfair. Every time we change the rules, he's more confused. Soon, he's is as neurotic as his masters.

Likewise, some people have a keen sense of fairness. Take my wife, Loretta, for example. She respects rules and boundaries, and she expects people to honor the boundaries they set and the rules *they* put into play. When people arbitrarily change the rules or randomly move the boundaries, it perplexes her. She lives by the golden rule: *Do unto others as you would have them do unto you.*

The reason dogs are compatible with people is because they mirror our feelings. Dogs have every emotion people have: love, anger, shame, envy, jealousy, regret, joy, fear... Everything we feel, they feel. They're empathetic. When we're sad, they're sad. When we're happy, they're happy.

In this respect, if people were more like dogs, society would be better off. Dogs are respectful. Dogs are loyal. Dogs respond to love. Dogs like playing by the rules, and they accept correction if it's fair.

SUMMARY

If Money were a person, he would be a college graduate – maybe a star athlete. He would be someone who understands rules, protocol, and social etiquette. He would be a high achiever, and he would be drawn to people of the same stripe.

If we want to go dog-fishing for people who are like Money, we must be respectful of their high values. They're not snobbish – they're well behaved. They're not elitist –

they're well bred. We'll never win the Money types if we're superficial. They're expert judges of human character.

We won't catch this kind of person with razzmatazz. We must be transparent and, above all, consistent. If we're the least bit wishy-washy, they'll be turned off. On the other hand, they'll honor loyalty with loyalty and integrity with integrity. Once we win their trust, we'll make a friend for life.

Money was our loving family member and a faithful friend until his last breath.

" **Money can buy you a fine dog, but only love can make his tail wag.**

— Kinky Friedman

A NOTE FROM THE AUTHOR...

I hope this little book, with a funny title, will spark you to remember we are all fishers of humanity – no matter what culture, nationality, or gender. With a little effort and understanding, people can be won for God.

To purchase other books or resources by Dick Bernal, visit www.jubilee.org.

Made in the USA
San Bernardino, CA
24 October 2017